Climate change is already affecting wildlife all over the planet.

Without urgent action, the Earth will continue to feel the effects of global warming. In the Arctic, sea temperatures are rising causing sea ice to melt and sea levels to rise. Polar animals, whose icy natural habitat is melting, are at risk of losing their homes and facing starvation.

You can help by taking action to save the Earth.

Lhinsey

'When we start to act hope is everywhere. So instead of looking for hope - look for action. Then the hope will come.' - Greta Thunberg

A Melting Planet is written and illustrated by Yasmin Kinsey.
Printed on green certified paper sourced from sustainable forests.
This is a first edition printed in 2019 in the UK. It is published by
Cambridge Children's Books, Cambridge, United Kingdom.

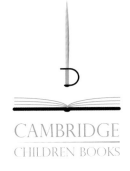

CAMBRIDGE
CHILDREN BOOKS

A
MELTING
PLANET

by Yasmin Kinsey

This is Pip the polar bear. She lives in the icy Arctic with her mum and little brother.

The sea temperature is rising causing the ice to melt.

Pip and her family like to play on the ice.

One day the ice suddenly **cracks** and the family is pulled apart.

Pip starts to drift away.

All alone,

Pip searches for her mum, but all she can see is

the deep blue sea.

Splash, a little seal pops out of the sea.

"My name is Sammy", said the little seal.

"Please come and sit with me", shouts Pip,

who does not want to be alone.

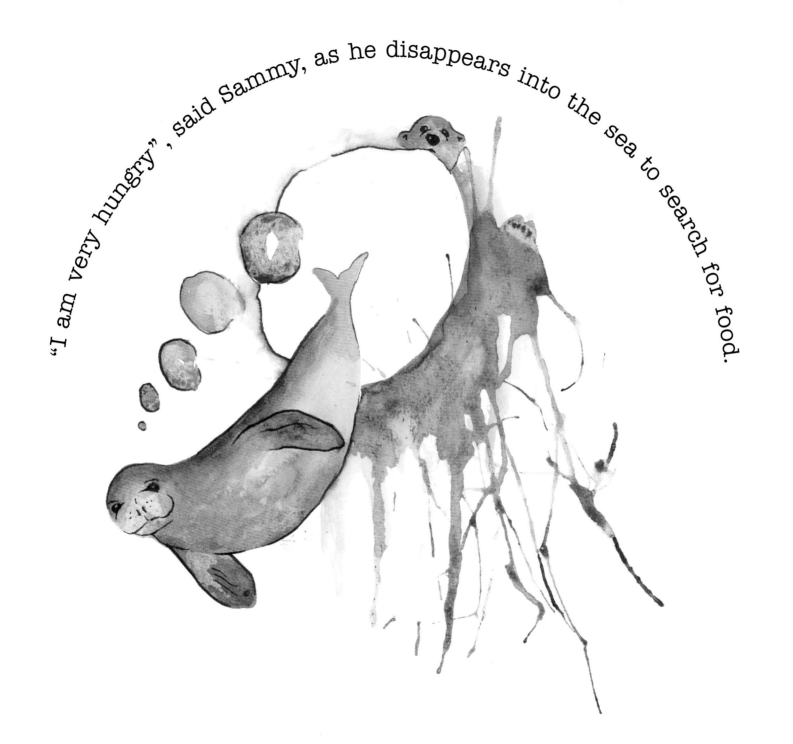

"I am very hungry", said Sammy, as he disappears into the sea to search for food.

Sammy cannot find any food.

The two new hungry friends sit side by side on the ice.

They start to feel worried.

A single shiny egg drifts towards them.

Where did it come from?

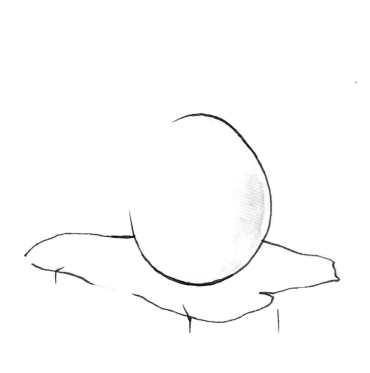

Pip and Sammy begin to feel hopeful as they float across the sea with the mysterious egg.

Hop, hop, hop.

Pip sees a colourful old hare jumping across the ice.

"Please help, I cannot swim", said the old hare.

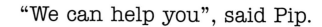

"We can help you", said Pip.

"Thank you, my name is Florence", said the old hare.

Huddled together, they float further and further

across the deep blue sea.

In the distance they see an arctic fox balancing on a small piece of ice. It is slowly melting away.

"Eeeek, he will surely eat us", squeaked Florence.

Wobble, wobble, wobble.

"Let me jump onto your ice. If you help me, I promise I will not eat you", said the arctic fox.

The new friends move in closer and the arctic fox leaps onto their ice. "Thank you, thank you, my name is Raven", said the arctic fox.

With her new friends by her side, Pip continues her unexpected adventure with hope and courage.

Suddenly, a **whale** rises out of the water.

There is a **huge wave.**

The wave breaks the ice and Pip falls into the sea.

The ice breaks up into even smaller

pieces. Pip tries to

keep swimming,

but she is getting tired.

Raven protects the mysterious egg
with his warm, furry tail.

The animals are lifted out of the sea onto the whales back.

The whale has come to rescue them.

One by one, the animals help each other onto a large ice shelf.

"Thank you Mr Whale",

shout the animals, as the whale returns to the deep blue sea.

Pip hears someone yelling...

"Pip, Pip, Pip!"

She sees her mum and little brother and they run towards each other.

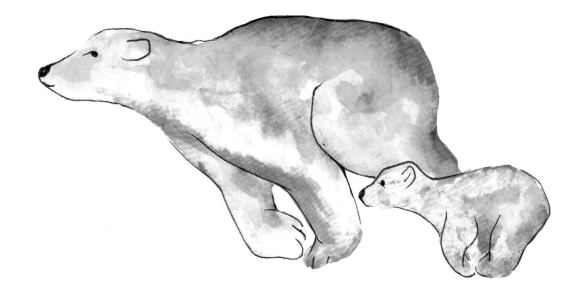

The family is reunited.

Crack, crack, crack.

The mysterious egg hatches

and a baby penguin is born.

"How did you get here?
You should be on the other side of
the world!" gasps Pip's mum.

"I will call you Hope", she said.

Pip is back with
her family...

... now her family is
bigger.

You can help save the planet.

If you follow these simple steps...

- Turn off lights and switch to energy saving bulbs.

- Recycle plastic, metal, glass, paper and reduce food waste.

- Turn off the tap while you are brushing your teeth.

- Use less plastic and use reusable bags when you go shopping.

- Walk, cycle or use public transport instead of travelling by car.

- Turn off the TV and computer when you do not need them.

- Plant a tree.